Jimmy Tarbuck Biography

JIMMY TARBUCK
BIOGRAPHY

LAUGHING THROUGH LIFE

THARIN LOCKEVE

Jimmy Tarbuck Biography

Copyright © **THARIN LOCKEVE** ,2025.

All rights reserved. No part of this publication may be reproduced,distributed,or transmitted in any form or by any means,including photocopying,recording, or other electronic or mechanical methods,without the prior written permission of the publisher,except in the case of brief quotations embodied in critical reviews and certain other noncommercial uses permitted by copyright law.

DISCLAIMER

The following book is for entertainment and informational purposes only. The information presented is without contract or any type of guarantee assurance. While every caution has been taken to provide accurate and current information, it is solely the reader's responsibility to check all information contained in this article before relying upon it.

Neither the author nor publisher can be held accountable for any errors or omissions. Under no circumstances will any legal responsibility or blame be held against the author or publisher for any reparation, damages, or monetary loss due to the information presented, either directly or indirectly.

Jimmy Tarbuck Biography

TABLE OF CONTENT

INTRODUCTION

CHAPTER 1: BEGINNINGS IN LIVERPOOL

CHAPTER 2: BREAKING INTO ENTERTAINMENT

CHAPTER 3: RISING STAR OF VARIETY

CHAPTER 4: QUIZ SHOWS AND GAME NIGHTS

CHAPTER 5: A COMEDIAN'S JOURNEY ON STAGE

CHAPTER 6: PERSONAL LIFE OFF STAGE

CHAPTER 7: TRIALS AND CONTROVERSIES

CHAPTER 8: LATER CAREER REINVENTIONAND

CHAPTER 9: LEGACY OF LAUGHTER

CHAPTER 10: REFLECTIONS AND THE ROAD AHEAD

Jimmy Tarbuck Biography

INTRODUCTION

Jimmy Tarbuck once described comedy as a kind of "life insurance for the soul" — a way to meet the world with humor, resilience, and a twinkle in the eye.

Born in Liverpool in the early 1940s, he grew up in a working-class family, long before the glare of spotlights or the roar of audiences filled his days.

Yet even as a child, he carried with him a spark: a liveliness that made people laugh, a curiosity that asked, What's next?

In his journey from local clubs to national television, Jimmy didn't just become a comedian — he became a symbol of a golden era in British entertainment.

 His voice, quick with jokes and warm with sincerity, carried him through decades.

He hosted quiz shows, made people chuckle in theatres, and brought joy into millions of living rooms.

But the life of an entertainer is rarely simple. Behind the laughter lay personal struggles, public scrutiny, and the weight of expectations.

Jimmy's story is one of triumphs and trials: of soaring to fame when television was king, of controversies that threatened to define him, and of reinvention when the world around him changed.

This book is not just a tribute; it's a conversation. It's a journey through the laughter, the silence, the bright lights, and the quiet moments when he reflects on who he was, where he came from, and what it all meant.

Jimmy Tarbuck Biography

From Liverpool to the limelight, Jimmy's path weaves through friendships and heartbreaks, through scandal and redemption, and ultimately, through a commitment to doing what he loved most: making people smile.

In the chapters that follow, you'll travel with Jimmy — backstage in crowded theatres, behind the camera in television studios, across green golf courses, and into the quiet rooms of memory.

You'll meet the people who shaped him, the moments that broke him, and the force he became as he held laughter in his hands and offered it to the world.

CHAPTER 1: BEGINNINGS IN LIVERPOOL

A Liverpudlian Birth and Family Roots

Jimmy Tarbuck was born in Wavertree, Liverpool, on 6 February 1940, into a modest working-class family. His father, Joseph Tarbuck, was a bookmaker, while his mother, Ada, kept the family grounded and supported her children through challenging times.

Jimmy had siblings, including a brother, Kenneth, and a sister, Norma. Tragically, another brother passed away when Jimmy was only a toddler.

Growing up in post-war Liverpool shaped him profoundly. The city, vibrant yet marked by economic struggle, instilled in him resilience and resourcefulness. Family life and close-knit community bonds offered a stable foundation, which nurtured his curiosity and early sense of humor.

School Days and Early Friendships

Jimmy's education began in local primary schools, where he first displayed his playful wit and love of attention. Among his schoolmates was a young John Lennon, with whom he shared a friendly camaraderie. Later, Jimmy attended secondary school, where strict discipline sometimes clashed with his mischievous nature, leading to occasional expulsion.

It was during a school play that Jimmy discovered the thrill of performing. Playing a comical role with his family cheering from the audience, he realized he could captivate others with humor. These early experiences planted the seeds for a lifelong career in entertainment.

Early Work and the First Taste of the Stage

After leaving school, Jimmy held a variety of jobs, including working as a mechanic and laborer. While none of these roles satisfied his ambitions, each taught him lessons in perseverance and adaptability.

At the age of 18, a turning point arrived when he participated in a talent contest at a holiday camp.

His charm, quick wit, and natural comedic timing impressed audiences and judges alike, and he soon found opportunities to perform in touring shows. These experiences marked the beginning of his journey into professional entertainment.

CHAPTER 2: BREAKING INTO ENTERTAINMENT

The First Steps on Stage

After his early experiences performing at local talent contests and holiday camps, Jimmy Tarbuck realized that his future lay not in conventional jobs but in entertaining others. His natural charisma, quick wit, and warmth made him a favorite among audiences even in small venues.

He began performing in local clubs and theaters, refining his comedic timing and learning to read the crowd. Each performance was a classroom in itself, teaching him the rhythm, improvisation, and connection that would define his style.

These early gigs were far from glamorous. Jimmy would travel long distances for modest pay, performing to audiences that were sometimes indifferent or challenging. Yet each stage became an opportunity to test new material, experiment with delivery, and build confidence.

The grit and persistence of these formative years laid the foundation for a career that would span decades.

Television Debut and Early Recognition

Jimmy's transition from stage to screen marked a pivotal moment in his career. He began making appearances on local television programs, where his energy and charm stood out.

Audiences responded positively, and producers began to notice his potential as a television personality.

Television offered a new kind of challenge. Unlike live theater, where reactions were immediate, the camera required precision, timing, and an awareness of the broader audience.

Jimmy adapted quickly, bringing the same warmth and humor that had won over club-goers to the small screen.

These early broadcasts were critical in establishing his reputation as a rising star in British entertainment.

Crafting a Persona: The Wit and Charm

From his first performances, Jimmy understood that success in entertainment depended not only on talent but on personality.

He cultivated a public persona that combined humor, approachability, and intelligence. Quick with a joke, clever in observation, yet never mean-spirited, he carved a niche that allowed him to appeal to a wide audience.

Beyond his comedic abilities, Jimmy's authenticity set him apart. Audiences sensed that he was not just performing a role but sharing a part of himself, his perspective, and his experiences.

This balance of personal engagement and professional skill became a defining characteristic of his career, helping him secure opportunities on larger stages and more prominent television programs.

CHAPTER 3: RISING STAR OF VARIETY

The Palladium Era and Big Breaks

As Jimmy Tarbuck gained experience on stage and television, he began to attract attention from producers and promoters who recognized his unique ability to charm and entertain. The 1960s were a golden era for variety shows, and Jimmy found himself stepping onto some of the most prestigious stages in the country.

One defining moment was his involvement with high-profile variety shows that drew large audiences. Performing in these arenas was both exhilarating and intimidating.

Each show demanded versatility: one moment he would be telling a joke, the next performing a quick sketch or interacting with the audience.

These appearances showcased not only his comedic talent but his confidence and poise under pressure, establishing him as a performer capable of commanding large venues.

Touring and Live Performances

While television provided exposure, live performances remained central to Jimmy's growth as a comedian.

He embarked on extensive tours, performing in theaters, clubs, and special events across the country.

These tours were physically demanding but creatively rewarding.

Touring allowed him to experiment with his routines, gauge audience reactions, and refine his timing. It was on these stages that he learned the subtleties of crowd engagement: how to read a room, adjust pacing, and balance humor with storytelling.

His commitment to connecting with audiences made him a reliable and sought-after performer in the variety circuit.

Building Relationships and Mentorships

During this period, Jimmy also formed important professional relationships.

Fellow entertainers, writers, and producers became allies and mentors, offering guidance and opportunities that would shape his career. At the same time, he became a mentor himself to younger performers, sharing insights about timing, delivery, and the nuances of stage presence.

These connections extended beyond the stage. Behind the scenes, he learned about show production, audience psychology, and the delicate balance between public persona and private life.

These lessons would serve him well as his fame grew and his career diversified into television, hosting, and other entertainment avenues.

CHAPTER 4: QUIZ SHOWS AND GAME NIGHTS

Transition to Television Hosting

By the 1970s, Jimmy Tarbuck had established himself as a versatile stage performer, but his charm and wit made him an ideal fit for television hosting. Producers recognized that his warmth, humor, and quick-thinking presence could translate seamlessly from live theater to the small screen.

Television offered a new challenge. Unlike performing for a live audience, where laughter and applause were immediate, hosting a quiz or game show required precise timing, engaging with contestants, and maintaining a lively pace that kept viewers at home entertained. Jimmy embraced this challenge, bringing his natural charisma and confidence into a format that required both structure and spontaneity.

Notable Programs and Defining Moments

Hosting quiz shows became one of the defining aspects of Jimmy's career. His approach was unique: he balanced humor with empathy, ensuring contestants felt comfortable while also keeping the audience captivated.

His style was approachable yet sharp, making viewers feel as though they were part of the experience.

Through these programs, Jimmy reached households across the nation. His presence in millions of living rooms turned him into a familiar figure, a trusted entertainer whose laughter became part of daily life for many. Each show, each segment, contributed to his growing reputation as not just a comedian, but a television personality capable of blending humor, intelligence, and charm.

Engaging the Public

What set Jimmy apart as a host was his ability to connect with people. Contestants, audiences, and viewers sensed authenticity.

He didn't rely solely on scripted lines or rehearsed jokes; he improvised, observed, and reacted, creating moments that were memorable and genuine.

This connection extended beyond television. Jimmy's persona became emblematic of a certain kind of light-hearted, relatable entertainment that balanced wit with kindness. People tuned in not just for the games themselves, but for the personality he brought, a personality that felt familiar, welcoming, and distinctly human.

CHAPTER 5: A COMEDIAN'S JOURNEY ON STAGE

Crafting a Unique Stand-Up Style

While television brought Jimmy Tarbuck widespread recognition, live performance remained the core of his identity as a comedian. On stage, he could fully express his humor, improvisation, and storytelling skills without the constraints of a scripted show.

Jimmy's style evolved over time, blending sharp observational humor with personal anecdotes and a gentle, self-deprecating wit.

He developed a rhythm that combined quick one-liners with longer stories, keeping audiences engaged while showcasing his personality. This careful balance between preparation and spontaneity became a hallmark of his performances, earning him respect among peers and affection from fans.

Touring, Residencies, and Special Performances

Touring was both challenging and rewarding. Jimmy traveled extensively across the country, performing in theaters, concert halls, and clubs of all sizes. Each venue presented a new audience, each night a new set of reactions to gauge and respond to.

Residencies allowed him to refine routines and experiment with new material in a controlled environment, while special performances, such as charity events or one-off shows, pushed him to adapt to varied audiences.

The experience of performing night after night, in diverse settings, honed his ability to read crowds, adjust pacing, and sustain energy over long periods.

Connecting with the Audience

Jimmy's success as a live performer stemmed from more than just clever jokes; it was his ability to connect with audiences on a personal level.

He understood the subtle cues of laughter, the pauses that made punchlines land, and the importance of authenticity in creating a shared experience.

Audiences were drawn not just to his humor but to his warmth. Jimmy's presence on stage felt inclusive, making people laugh while feeling seen and appreciated. Over time, this connection became a defining characteristic of his live shows, earning him loyal fans and cementing his reputation as one of the most engaging comedians of his generation.

CHAPTER 6: PERSONAL LIFE OFF STAGE

Marriage, Family, and Home Life

Behind the laughter and applause, Jimmy Tarbuck's personal life was anchored by his family. He married Pauline Carfoot in 1959, a partnership that would endure through decades of both professional highs and personal challenges. Together, they built a home that reflected stability, warmth, and support — qualities that would provide Jimmy with a grounding counterpoint to the unpredictable world of entertainment.

Their family life included raising three children, among them Liza Tarbuck, who would go on to carve her own path in television and radio. Jimmy often credited his family for keeping him grounded, emphasizing that while public life could be demanding and fast-paced, his home was a sanctuary where laughter and love were constants.

Passions Beyond the Stage

Outside of show business, Jimmy had interests that reflected his personality and provided balance. Golf became a lifelong passion, a sport that combined skill, patience, and camaraderie. Many evenings and weekends were spent on the green, offering both relaxation and a sense of competition separate from the world of entertainment.

In addition to golf, Jimmy had an interest in politics and social issues, expressing views that were informed by personal experience and a desire to engage with the broader world. Though his political opinions sometimes sparked discussion, they were always delivered with the same wit and thoughtfulness that characterized his public persona.

Balancing Fame and Privacy

Fame brought attention, but also challenges in maintaining personal privacy. Jimmy learned early that the public eye could intrude, and he developed strategies to protect his family's space while remaining accessible to fans.

This balance required negotiation and discipline, as the pressures of a career in entertainment could otherwise overshadow personal life.

Maintaining strong family ties and pursuing personal interests allowed Jimmy to navigate the highs and lows of a public career with perspective.

The lessons of balance, resilience, and prioritizing meaningful relationships would prove invaluable throughout his life.

CHAPTER 7: TRIALS AND CONTROVERSIES

Facing Public Scrutiny

No life in the spotlight is without challenges, and Jimmy Tarbuck's career was no exception. Despite decades of success, he faced moments of public scrutiny that tested both his resilience and his reputation. Being a well-known entertainer meant that his every action, past and present, could be examined under a critical lens.

This scrutiny was amplified by the media, which often sought sensational stories. Jimmy had to navigate these pressures carefully, balancing honesty with discretion, and learning that public perception could be both supportive and harsh. His ability to remain composed under these conditions was a testament to his experience and character.

Legal and Personal Challenges

Throughout his life, Jimmy encountered legal and personal challenges that became widely reported. One notable episode involved historic allegations that, while serious in nature, ultimately did not result in charges or convictions. Jimmy faced these allegations with dignity, maintaining his innocence and cooperating fully with authorities.

In addition, he experienced minor legal incidents, such as a traffic offense, which highlighted the fact that even minor mistakes could attract public attention for someone of his profile. These experiences reinforced the importance of personal accountability and the constant need to navigate life with care, particularly under the scrutiny that comes with fame.

Resilience Through Adversity

What set Jimmy apart during these difficult times was his resilience. He drew strength from his family, his close circle of friends, and his passion for performance.

Humor became not just a profession but a tool for coping and maintaining perspective.

Even when facing controversy, he remained committed to his craft and to the people who supported him.

He understood that public missteps or false allegations could be temporary, but the relationships, integrity, and work ethic he had cultivated over decades were lasting. This ability to persevere helped him weather storms that might have derailed a lesser career.

CHAPTER 8: LATER CAREER REINVENTIONAND

Embracing New Opportunities

As Jimmy Tarbuck moved into the later stages of his career, the entertainment landscape was changing. Television formats evolved, audiences shifted, and new performers emerged, bringing fresh energy and competition. Rather than resisting change, Jimmy embraced new opportunities, adapting his style to fit contemporary tastes while remaining true to his signature humor.

He appeared on talk shows, variety specials, and charity events, often demonstrating versatility that few performers could match. Each appearance was a chance to reconnect with long-time fans and introduce himself to a younger generation. This adaptability became a defining trait, allowing him to remain relevant in an industry that often forgets its veterans.

Returning to the Stage

While television offered exposure, Jimmy always found a sense of fulfillment on stage. In the later years, he returned to theaters and live performances, often revisiting material from earlier in his career while incorporating new insights and experiences.

These performances were not simply nostalgic; they were opportunities to showcase a performer who had honed his craft over decades. Audiences appreciated not only the jokes but the depth, timing, and warmth that came from years of experience.

His ability to sustain energy and engagement over long tours or special shows underscored the enduring quality of his talent.

Reinventing the Persona

Reinvention was not about changing who he was but evolving his public persona to match new expectations.

Jimmy became more reflective in interviews, sharing stories from his life with humor and insight.

He balanced playful mischief with the wisdom gained from decades in the spotlight.

By embracing this evolution, he demonstrated that longevity in entertainment depends not solely on talent but on self-awareness, openness to growth, and the willingness to step outside comfort zones. Reinvention allowed him to remain a beloved figure while exploring new dimensions of his career.

CHAPTER 9: LEGACY OF LAUGHTER

Influence on Younger Comedians

Jimmy Tarbuck's impact on British entertainment extends far beyond his own performances. Through his distinctive style, professionalism, and approachability, he became a model for younger comedians entering the field. Many performers have cited his timing, stage presence, and ability to connect with audiences as key influences in shaping their own careers.

He demonstrated that humor could be both intelligent and accessible, blending quick-witted observations with warmth and charm. By showing that comedy could be versatile—equally effective on stage, television, or live events—Jimmy set a standard for future generations, illustrating how entertainers could adapt without losing authenticity.

Contributions to Entertainment and Culture

Beyond mentorship, Jimmy's body of work contributed significantly to the culture of entertainment. He brought variety shows, quiz shows, and live performances into the homes and hearts of millions.

His ability to make audiences laugh while maintaining a genuine connection helped to elevate the role of the comedian in public life.

Through his television appearances and stage performances, he helped shape the expectations of audiences and producers alike. The warmth, wit, and professionalism he consistently demonstrated contributed to a standard of excellence in British entertainment, leaving a mark that continues to be recognized today.

Recognition and Public Appreciation

Jimmy Tarbuck's contributions have been acknowledged through awards, honors, and the enduring admiration of the public. Fans remember not only the jokes but the personality behind them: approachable, humorous, and resilient. Public affection has remained a constant, reflecting the impact of a performer who successfully balanced humor with authenticity.

Even in his later years, Jimmy continued to engage audiences, whether through stage performances, television specials, or public appearances.

His enduring presence illustrates that a comedian's influence is not limited to the immediate laughter they create but extends to the inspiration and enjoyment they leave behind.

CHAPTER 10: REFLECTIONS AND THE ROAD AHEAD

Personal Reflections on Life and Career

As Jimmy Tarbuck looks back on his life, a clear theme emerges: humor has been both his vocation and his guiding philosophy. From the streets of Liverpool to the bright lights of television studios and theater stages, he has relied on laughter to navigate challenges, connect with people, and leave a lasting impression.

Jimmy often reflects on the lessons learned along the way. Early failures, missteps, and personal challenges were not setbacks but opportunities for growth.

He emphasizes the importance of perseverance, adaptability, and staying true to oneself. His career demonstrates that talent alone is insufficient; success also requires determination, humility, and an ability to embrace change.

Lessons Learned and Words of Wisdom

Through decades of experience, Jimmy has accumulated wisdom that extends beyond comedy. He highlights the value of authenticity: audiences respond to honesty, sincerity, and a performer's willingness to share a piece of themselves. Equally important is resilience—facing public scrutiny, legal challenges, or personal struggles with composure, humor, and reflection.

Jimmy encourages younger performers to remain curious, embrace challenges, and cultivate relationships both on and off stage. He underscores that the bonds formed, the lessons learned, and the respect earned often outlast the applause of any particular performance.

Humor, he notes, is not just entertainment; it is a bridge that fosters connection, empathy, and joy.

Looking Toward the Future

Even as he moves into the later chapters of his life, Jimmy remains engaged with audiences and the world of entertainment. Whether through occasional stage performances, television appearances, or mentoring emerging talent, he continues to share his passion and insight.

The road ahead is as much about legacy as it is about personal fulfillment. Jimmy Tarbuck's life story reminds us that careers can evolve, challenges can be met with courage, and humor can remain a sustaining force. As he reflects on the past and considers what lies ahead, one constant remains: the ability to make people laugh, think, and feel connected—a gift he has shared generously throughout his remarkable life.

CONCLUSION

The Enduring Spirit of Laughter

Jimmy Tarbuck's life is a testament to the power of humor, resilience, and authenticity. From his humble beginnings in Liverpool to commanding stages and television studios across the country, he built a career that touched millions of lives. His journey was never a straight path; it was filled with challenges, public scrutiny, and personal trials. Yet through it all, laughter remained his constant companion and guiding force.

What makes Jimmy's story remarkable is not only the applause he earned but the connections he forged along the way. Whether engaging a live audience, hosting a quiz show, or mentoring young comedians, he demonstrated that entertainment is about more than performance—it is about empathy, joy, and shared experience.

In reflecting on his career and life, one sees a man who remained true to himself, who embraced change without losing his essence, and who understood the delicate balance between public persona and private life.

His legacy is not only in the laughter he created but in the example he set for perseverance, professionalism, and warmth.

Jimmy Tarbuck's story reminds us that life, like comedy, is a journey best traveled with resilience, humor, and heart. It teaches that even in moments of challenge, the ability to find lightness and connection can leave a lasting mark—not just on audiences, but on the world.

In the end, the laughter continues. And through it, Jimmy Tarbuck's spirit lives on, inspiring all who encounter his story to embrace life with courage, wit, and joy.

THE END

Printed in Dunstable, United Kingdom